TIGERS

LIVING WILD

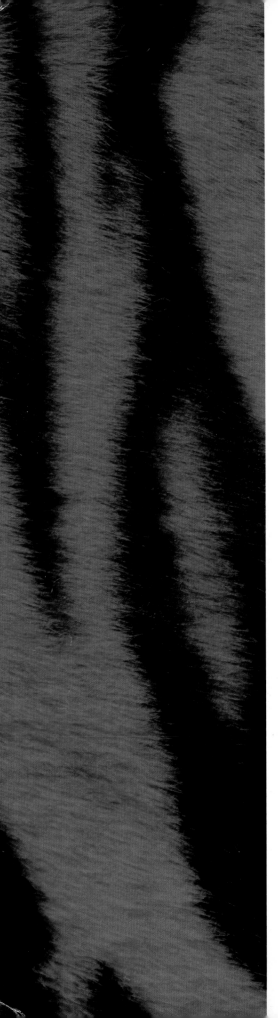

LIVING WILD

Published by Creative Education

P.O. Box 227, Mankato, Minnesota 56002

Creative Education is an imprint of The Creative Company

Design and production by Mary Herrmann

Art direction by Rita Marshall

Printed in the United States of America

Photographs by Dreamstime (Jedendva, Napy8gen), Getty Images (After Anonio Niccolini, Theo Allofs, Altrendo Nature, Chris Baker, Jason Edwards, Hulton Archive, ALEXANDER JOE/AFP, P. Kumar, Thorsten Milse, Michael K. Nichols/National Geographic, Joe Robbins, Anup Shah, Harri Tahvanainen, Gary Vestal, Renaud Visage, Art Wolfe, Zhinong Xi), iStockphoto (Kitch Bain, Vinod Bartakk, Robb Broek, Barry Crossley, Derek Dammann, Hanafi Jamil, Keith Livingston, Ryan Lusher, Neal McClimon, Stephen Meese, Dawn Nichols, Gino Santa Maria)

Library of Congress Cataloging-in-Publication Data

Hanel, Rachael.

Tigers / by Rachael Hanel.

p. cm. — (Living wild)

Includes index.

ISBN 978-1-58341-660-0

1. Tigers—Juvenile literature. I. Title. II. Series.

QL737.C23H353 2008

599.756—dc22   2007008504

9 8 7 6 5 4 3 2

CREATIVE EDUCATION

TIGERS

Rachael Hanel

The tiger settles into the tall grass
for a nap and closes his eyes.

Just as he starts to doze off,
he hears a noise several yards away.

The tiger settles into the tall grass for a nap and closes his eyes. Just as he starts to doze off, he hears a noise several yards away. His eyes snap open, and only his head jerks up; he is careful not to reveal himself. His sharp eyes focus on the nearby watering hole. There, sipping gently, is a deer-like sambar. The tiger is hungry; the sambar would make a good meal. The tiger crouches low to the ground, his muscles as tense as loaded springs. He inches forward, belly close to the ground. He is so quiet that the sambar does not hear a thing. When the tiger comes close enough to his prey, he leaps several feet out of the grass and grabs his victim. After a short struggle, the sambar is dead. The tiger drags the body to a well-hidden place and eats. His hunger will be satisfied for a few more days.

WHERE IN THE WORLD THEY LIVE

☐ **Sumatran Tiger**
Indonesian island
of Sumatra

☐ **IndoChinese Tiger**
Thailand,
Cambodia,
Vietnam, China,
and other parts
of Southeast Asia

☐ **Bengal Tiger**
southern Asia,
especially India

■ **Siberian Tiger**
far eastern Asia
(northern China,
North Korea,
and Russia)

☐ **Malayan Tiger**
southern part
of the Malay
Peninsula

☐ **South China Tiger**
southeastern
China

Of the six tiger subspecies that live in the world today, all except the Siberian are found in the southeastern parts of Asia. The colored dots represent the native territories of tigers that continue to live in the wild.

THE LARGEST CAT

The majestic tiger is the largest member of the Felidae, or cat, family. Tigers can weigh up to 660 pounds (300 kg) and stretch 11 feet (3.3 m) from head to tail. Even the mighty lion, with its thick mane and strong body, is smaller than the tiger. Tigers rule over a family that also includes leopards, cheetahs, and house cats. The tiger's scientific name is *Panthera tigris*.

There are six subspecies of tiger, but all share common characteristics that make the animal distinctive and allow it to survive in its environment. The brown-orange fur lined with bold black or brown stripes helps a tiger stay **camouflaged** when surrounded by tall grass and thick forests. This allows tigers to sneak up on prey undetected.

The tiger's thick leg muscles help it chase prey on land and even climb short distances up trees. Its paws look like much larger versions of house cats' paws. Soft pads on the bottom of the paws help it to walk quietly. When not in use, a tiger's claws **retract** into its paws. The claws are used for attacking prey or other tigers. To keep claws sharp, a tiger will scratch them on a tree trunk. Tigers use the force of their large paws to

Just as each human has a unique fingerprint, each tiger sports a unique pattern of stripes. This helps researchers tell them apart.

Tigers in captivity may eat at any time of the day and do not have to hunt their prey at night.

A tiger's body contains more than 600 muscles, which gives it the power and agility needed to hunt large prey.

knock small prey off their feet, like a boxer delivering a knockout punch.

One of the tiger's most powerful features is its large jaws. A tiger has 30 teeth. Four long teeth called canines jut out of the jawbone, two on top and two on bottom. These teeth, which are about three inches (7.6 cm) long, look like fangs and are used to bite into prey. The back teeth, called carnassials, are jagged and sharp and help a tiger rip meat apart.

Tigers are nocturnal animals, which means they like to hunt and travel at night. They gaze intently on their world with bright, yellow eyes. Tigers can see up to six times better than humans at night, and this helps them expertly track their prey. Tigers also have strong senses of hearing and smell.

Tigers are found throughout Asia: from the cold landscapes of eastern Russia and northern China to the steamy jungles of the island of Sumatra, and from the dry forests and mountains of India to the rivers of Cambodia. Tigers need three things to survive—a water source, such as a pond or river; places to hide, such as tall grass, rock outcroppings, or forests; and plenty of prey to eat. Each

Growling is one way a tiger warns other animals or people that they have crossed into its territory.

Tigers that live in grassy areas close to forests have an advantage in stalking their prey under cover.

species of tiger is suited to a particular region because of its fur, coloring, and body size.

The most common tigers are Bengals. These tigers are found in the dry forests and Himalayan mountain regions of India, Nepal, Bangladesh, Bhutan, and Myanmar. Male Bengals are about 9 and a half feet (2.9 m) long and weigh up to 480 pounds (220 kg); the females are slightly smaller. The fringe of white hair around a Bengal tiger's face is longer than in other species.

Much more difficult to find is a completely white tiger with blue eyes and brown stripes. This beautiful white tiger is not a separate subspecies but is a rare form of the Bengal tiger. White tigers live in captivity and have not been reported seen in the wild since the 1950s. Their color makes it impossible to hide from predators, so they do not survive for long.

The Siberian tiger is the largest species, with males growing to nearly 11 feet (3 m) long and weighing up to 660 pounds (300 kg). These tigers are covered with thick fur because of where they live—the cold regions of Russia and northern China. The Siberian tiger's large body helps it retain more heat, and the fur acts as

Ohio's Cincinnati Zoo holds the largest population of white Bengal tigers in the world today.

insulation against the temperatures and wind. The fur of a Siberian tiger is paler than that of other tigers, and its belly is entirely white. This helps the Siberian tiger to stay hidden in its habitat, which is often covered in snow. Its stripes are brown, rather than black, and they are spaced widely apart.

In Thailand, the IndoChinese tiger dominates. It is also found in Myanmar, Vietnam, China, Cambodia, and Laos. It is smaller than the Bengal tiger, averaging about 9 feet (2.7 m) in length and weighing up to 400 pounds (180 kg). Its fur is a bit darker than average, and its stripes are shorter and spaced closely together.

The Sumatran tiger is found only in Sumatra, a forested island of Indonesia. It is the smallest subspecies, with the male averaging about 8 feet (2.5 m) in length and weighing about 260 pounds (120 kg). It has the darkest coat of all tigers, and its stripes are spaced closely together and extend down the forelegs.

The rarest tiger is the South China tiger, with only a couple dozen still living in the wild. The last reported sighting of one occurred in 1999. The South China tiger averages the same length as the Sumatran but weighs

Siberian tigers are at home in their snowy habitats but often migrate to find sufficient food.

Unlike most cats, tigers enjoy bathing and often swim to cool off during periods of warmer weather.

up to 330 pounds (150 kg). This species has short, broad stripes that are spaced far apart.

In 2004, scientists discovered a new subspecies: the Malayan tiger. This tiger is found on the southern tip of Thailand and the Malaysian peninsula and is similar in size to the Sumatran tiger.

Unlike most cats, tigers enjoy being in the water. Because many tigers live in hot climates, they will wade into a pond or river to stay cool. Tigers are good

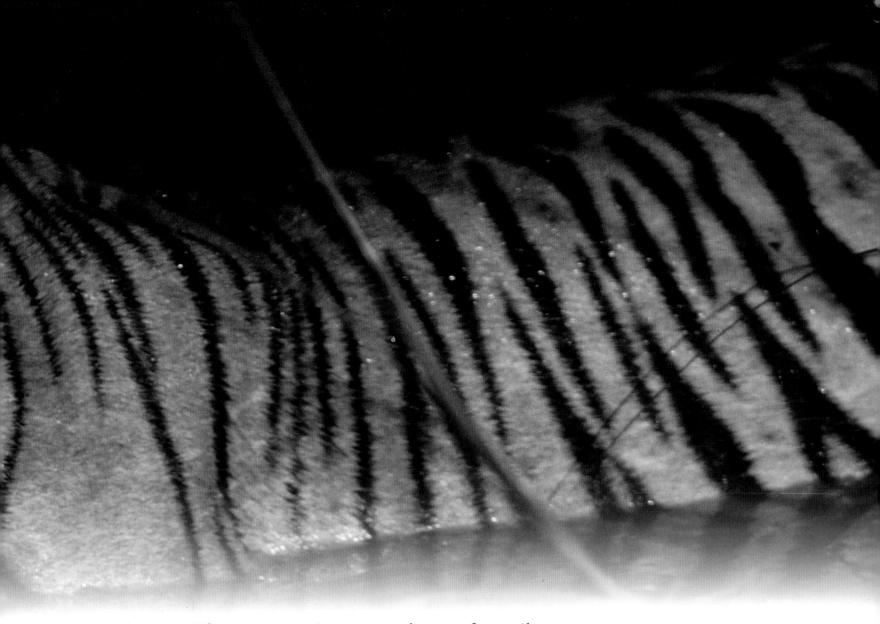

swimmers. They can sometimes cover three to four miles (4.8–6.4 km) of a river at one time.

The size of a tiger's territory depends on the number of prey animals within it. In more isolated regions, such as Russia or China, a tiger might roam more than 135 square miles (350 sq km) to find an adequate supply of food. Where tigers and prey are more abundant, such as in India, their territory might cover only 10 square miles (26 sq km).

Bengal tigers in India will sometimes eat monkeys such as the gray langur.

A SOLITARY LIFE

tiger's life, for the most part, is relaxing. It spends 18 to 20 hours of its day resting or sleeping. But when a tiger is on the move, especially on a hunt, that is when the animal springs into action.

Tigers are carnivores, which means they eat mostly meat. On the flat plains of Russia and northern China, the Siberian tiger preys upon an elk–like animal called a wapiti. In the jungles, tigers eat monkeys. And in the dry forests of India, tigers most often eat wild boar, peacocks, and wild cattle, along with the sambar. If they are desperate for food, they will eat frogs, crabs, fish, and even porcupines.

Tigers know that water sources are the best places to find prey because all animals must drink. During the day, a hungry tiger will rest and hide near a river or pond. Sometimes tigers will hunt during the day, but they prefer to stalk prey under the cover of darkness. When the time is right, a tiger will silently inch closer to its target until it is about 65 feet (20 m) away. As soon as it gets near enough, it crouches and then leaps to attack. Once a tiger lands on its target, it sinks its long canine teeth into the

Although tigers do not have manes, a tiger's age can show in how long the hairs of its cheeks get.

In order to survive, a tiger needs to eat the equivalent of one deer-sized animal per week. A tiger with cubs needs more than that.

animal's throat, cutting off its air and blood supply.

Since tigers are so big, it might seem that they could easily overpower and take down any animal. But a tiger's strength is also its greatest weakness. It is so large that it can run quickly for only short distances. A tiger's prey is usually smaller and lighter, and animals such as sambars use their swiftness to outrun a pursuing tiger. An animal such as a monkey can climb high into a tree, far out of the reach of a tiger's paws. Animals such as sambars and cattle live in herds, and they call out to each other when they sense danger. Tigers have to be persistent when stalking prey; it may take a tiger 20 tries before it gets a meal.

When a tiger makes a kill, it drags the **carcass** to a hiding spot in an area of dense vegetation or sheltering rocks. It does not want to share its meal with other tigers or other animals, and it can take a tiger several hours to gnaw through the meat. Its strong teeth allow it to rip through tough meat, and it will even snap and crush bones and eat them, too. A tiger will eat for only about an hour at a time before it gets tired and has to rest.

Like most cats (other than lions), tigers live by themselves. They mark their territories by urinating on trees and bushes. But often the territory of a male and female will overlap. In this case, the male and female will mate with each other. When a female is ready to mate, she uses her scent to attract males. She also roars and moans to let a male know she is ready. Tigers can mate any time during the year, but they usually prefer to do so during the cooler months.

Fast-growing tiger cubs get big enough to leave the protection of their mother within two years.

About three months after mating, the female tiger gives birth to a **litter** of two to six cubs. When she is ready to give birth, the mother finds a cool, dry hiding spot. This may be in a **den** such as a secluded area of tall grass. Here, her cubs will be protected from harsh weather and dangerous animals. The cubs are tiny; at birth, they weigh just two to three pounds (0.9–1.4 kg) and are completely helpless. Their eyes will not open for a week or two. They have no teeth; they get all their nourishment from their mother's milk. The mother licks her cubs clean so they will not give off any scent that would reveal their location.

At about six to eight weeks, the tigers have developed baby teeth and can start to eat meat their mothers bring back to the den. Finding enough food for both herself and her cubs exhausts the mother. She might have to leave the

Because of the extra loose skin around a cub's neck, its mother can safely carry it in her teeth.

den every day to find meat. While she is gone, the cubs rest quietly. But whenever they are alone, they are always in danger of being killed by other animals such as jackals and leopards. If a mother senses danger, she will grunt or make a squeaking noise to tell her cubs to stay close.

At around eight weeks old, cubs start to venture outside the den, but they are always under the watchful eyes of their mother. As the cubs playfully swat at and chase each other, they develop skills that will help them learn how to hunt. Once the cubs are several months old, the mother might let them finish off a kill after she has injured an animal. Only when tigers are about one and a half years old can they hunt on their own. By this time, their permanent teeth have come in, and they separate from their mother for longer periods of time. At two years old, the cubs are ready to live on their own. A female cub may stay with her mother a little longer than a male cub, but eventually all cubs leave to find their own territory. Brothers might stick together for a while, but they, too, will eventually go their separate ways.

Tigers sometimes take over a territory peacefully. If a tiger is old and dying, it will not put up a fight when

a younger tiger comes into its territory. But other times, tigers fight violently for space. They lash out at each other using their sharp claws, and sometimes one will kill the other. If a male tiger comes across cubs that are not his, he may kill them. Only about half of all cubs survive to adulthood, but those that do have a good chance of living about 10 to 15 years in the wild. In captivity, tigers can live for 16 to 20 years.

Male tigers will fight ferociously during deadly battles to protect the territory they have claimed.

In ancient Rome, captured and imported animals such as tigers were made to fight against humans in large arenas.

A CENTURY OF SUFFERING

Tigers and humans have a long, intertwined history. Tribal cultures of India and other parts of Asia honored the tiger by including it in their art for thousands of years. Historical records show that tigers were brought to Europe during the reign of Greek emperor Alexander the Great in the fourth century B.C. Alexander's rule extended into India, and he and his companions captured tigers there and brought them to Athens, Greece. In the Roman Empire of about 2,000 years ago, popular **gladiator** contests often featured matches between humans and tigers. In the 13th century, Italian adventurer Marco Polo encountered tigers on his travels to Asia and referred to them as "striped lions."

People have always hunted tigers for their meat, skin, and bones. However, these hunts killed isolated numbers of tigers and did not negatively affect their overall population. It was not until the use of firearms became widespread in the 18th century that tigers began to be killed in excessive numbers. Shooting tigers became a popular sport among the wealthy in the 19th century. During this time, European nations established **colonies**

Rome's Colosseum, built in the first century A.D., held thousands of gladiator combats and other sports.

In the 15th century, adventurers and explorers started bringing tigers back to Europe and placing them in early zoos called menageries.

Africa's Laohu Valley Reserve, home to a handful of South China tigers, is trying to save them from extinction.

throughout Asia. Europeans who traveled to and lived in Asia had never seen wildlife such as tigers, and they took great satisfaction and pride in killing the strong animals. Tiger hunting flourished among native upper classes and European colonial officials.

But it was the 20th century that proved most harmful to tiger populations. More than most animals, the tiger saw some of the biggest declines in its population in just one century. In the early 1900s, the global tiger population was estimated at 100,000. Tigers could be found as far west as Turkey and throughout Russia, Korea, and the Indonesian islands of Java and Bali.

After World War II ended in 1945, tiger populations—already on the decline for decades due to unchecked hunting practices—suffered even steeper declines for two primary reasons. The human population was growing rapidly and demanded land for villages, cities, and agriculture. To make room for human expansion, tigers were forced to compete among themselves for smaller territories. In addition, hunting became easier as people flew in from all over the world for the privilege of killing exotic animals such as tigers.

Smugglers can make a lot of money by illegally selling exotic animal skins such as those of tigers.

The Malayan tiger (above) shares many traits with the IndoChinese tiger.

All tigers have a patch of white on their ears. This helps them to spot each other even in dense grass or jungle landscapes.

Throughout the 20th century, government officials in Russia, China, and Indonesia actually paid people to kill tigers. As the human population expanded and infringed upon tiger territory, more tigers started to kill humans and domestic animals such as cattle and dogs. The tiger was seen as a threat, and **bounties** were placed on them. By the 1950s, tigers near the Caspian Sea in Russia were gone. By the 1960s, some tiger species had vanished completely, and total numbers declined to just 2,000 or so. In China, this practice of issuing bounties continued until 1977.

All tiger subspecies were declared endangered in 1969. In addition to the Caspian tiger, two other tiger subspecies no longer exist—the Balinese tiger, extinct by the 1940s, and the Javan tiger, extinct since the 1980s. These extinctions prompted conservation efforts to start in the 1970s, with the first large-scale effort occurring in India in 1973. Project Tiger established protected areas for the tiger throughout the country, and its numbers started to increase. But **poachers** found it easy to avoid conservation officers, and by the 1990s, the rise in illegal trading of tiger furs and body parts threatened the tiger population once again. Additionally, the human

population in India exploded around the same time, straining the boundaries of the preserves and pushing government resources to the limit. Livestock were often victims of tiger attacks, and farmers retaliated by killing tigers. It wasn't until the turn of the 21st century that Project Tiger was able to stem the threats posed by poachers and farmers.

A study released in 2006 found that tigers inhabited only seven percent of their historic range. Today, the big cats are found in just 13 countries. Efforts to save the tiger are working, and the population has climbed to

Tigers figure prominently in the art and legends of several Indian and Southeast Asian cultures.

MOWGLI'S SONG

I, Mowgli, am singing.

Let the jungle listen to the things I have done.

Shere Khan said he would kill—would kill!

At the gates in the twilight he would kill Mowgli, the Frog!

He ate and he drank. Drink deep,

Shere Khan, for when wilt thou drink again?

Sleep and dream of the kill.

I am alone on the grazing-grounds.

Gray Brother, come to me!

Come to me, Lone Wolf, for there is big game afoot.

Bring up the great bull-buffaloes, the blue-skinned herd-bulls
    with the angry eyes.

Drive them to and fro as I order.

Sleepest thou still, Shere Khan? Wake, O wake!

Here come I, and the bulls are behind.

Rama, the King of the Buffaloes, stamped with his foot.

Waters of the Waingunga, whither went Shere Khan?

He is not Ikki to dig holes, nor Mao, the Peacock,
    that he should fly.

He is not Mang, the Bat, to hang in the branches.

Little bamboos that creak together, tell me where he ran?

Ow! He is there. Ahoo! He is there.

Under the feet of Rama lies the Lame One! Up, Shere Khan!

Up and kill! Here is meat; break the necks of the bulls!

Hsh! He is asleep. We will not wake him, for his strength is
    very great.

The kites have come down to see it.

The black ants have come up to know it.

There is a great assembly in his honour.

Alala! I have no cloth to wrap me.

The kites will see that I am naked.

I am ashamed to meet all these people.

Lend me thy coat, Shere Khan. Lend me thy gay striped coat
    that I may go to the Council Rock.

By the Bull that bought me I have made a promise—
    a little promise.

Only thy coat is lacking before I keep my word.

With the knife—with the knife that men use—with the knife of
    the hunter, the man, I will stoop down for my gift.

Waters of the Waingunga, bear witness that Shere Khan gives me
    his coat for the love that he bears me.

Pull, Gray Brother! Pull, Akela! Heavy is the hide of Shere Khan.

The Man Pack are angry. They throw stones and talk child's talk.

My mouth is bleeding. Let us run away.

Through the night, through the hot night, run swiftly with me,
    my brothers.

We will leave the lights of the village and go to the low moon.

Waters of the Waingunga, the Man Pack have cast me out.

I did them no harm, but they were afraid of me. Why?

Wolf Pack, ye have cast me out too.

The jungle is shut to me and the village gates are shut. Why?

As Mang flies between the beasts and the birds so fly

I between the village and the jungle. Why?

I dance on the hide of Shere Khan, but my heart is very heavy.

My mouth is cut and wounded with the stones from the village, but
    my heart is very light because I have come back to the jungle.

Why?

These two things fight together in me as the snakes fight
    in the spring.

The water comes out of my eyes; yet I laugh while it falls. Why?

I am two Mowglis, but the hide of Shere Khan is under my feet.

All the jungle knows that I have killed Shere Khan.

Look—look well, O Wolves!

Ahae! My heart is heavy with the things that I do not understand.

Rudyard Kipling (1865–1936), The Jungle Book

between 5,000 and 7,000. Still, tigers face threats daily and are thought to live on 40 percent less land than they did only a decade ago.

Tigers, for all their dangerous mannerisms, have a **regal** air and can even appear cuddly, with their gentle eyes and soft fur. Throughout the 19th and 20th centuries, as more of the world became familiar with them, the animals were adopted into human culture across the globe.

Tigers have long made for popular characters in books, cartoons, and **logos**. Nineteenth-century British author Rudyard Kipling, who was born in India to British parents, published *The Jungle Book* in 1894. The stories within Kipling's book brought a whole new set of exotic creatures to life for young girls and boys. Kipling chose to portray the tiger, Shere Khan, as a mean and vicious villain who was always out to trick and eat the boy Mowgli.

Another British author, A. A. Milne, created a much friendlier tiger—named Tigger—for his book *Winnie the Pooh*, published in 1926. Tigger excitedly bounces through Milne's books alongside the characters of Pooh and Piglet. The fun-loving tiger starred in his own big-

Rudyard Kipling, made popular by his short stories, received the Nobel Prize for Literature in 1907.

screen adventure in 2000, *The Tigger Movie*, in which he sets out to find his family.

Tony the Tiger, the "spokes-animal" for Kellogg's cereal Frosted Flakes, is one of the best-known American advertising **icons**. The deep-voiced tiger beat out other potential mascots—such as a kangaroo and an elephant—for the job through a contest. Since 1952, Tony's famous, roaring line, "They're G-R-R-R-R-E-A-T!" has endeared him to generations of children.

Because tigers are powerful and can be fierce and competitive, they are popular choices as mascots for sports teams, both amateur and professional. In Major League Baseball, the Tigers of Detroit, Michigan, have used a tiger as their mascot since the turn of the 20th century. In the National Football League, the Cincinnati Bengals have tiger-striped helmets.

More than anyone else, Las Vegas entertainers Siegfried and Roy have made the white tiger famous. These magicians have used white tigers in their act since the 1980s, exposing thousands of people each year to the beauty and majesty of this rare animal.

Majestic tigers in their natural habitat (opposite) have inspired people to make many statues, such as this one at the Detroit Tigers' home stadium.

KNOWING THE TIGER

Scientists have been intrigued by tigers since the mid-1900s and continue to uncover new information about the animals' habitat requirements and behavior patterns. The *Panthera* cats—including tigers, lions, and jaguars—are thought to have branched away from the other Felidae cats five million years ago. Tigers likely originated in East Asia, and fossils of the early animals have been found that date from 500,000 to 2 million years old.

Tigers adapted and spread throughout Asia wherever prey and land were available. When the global climate was warmer and lower sea levels exposed land, they traveled to the Indonesian islands. Tiger fossils have also been found in Japan and on a land bridge that once existed between Asia and North America.

The first person to regularly study tigers in the wild was **conservationist** and **zoologist** George Schaller. This American scientist published the first book on tiger behavior, *The Deer and the Tiger,* in 1967. For months, he studied tigers and other animals in India's Kanha National Park. Schaller first observed many behaviors now commonly known about tigers. For example, he determined that tiger cubs suffer high mortality rates. He also noted that male tigers were highly territorial and competitive. In addition, Schaller observed tigers to be solitary creatures. Much of this early research helped later conservation efforts, since it was known how tigers behave socially, how much territory they need, and how many tigers need to be born in order to sustain a population.

Today, tiger research centers largely on the animal's ability to survive. Scientists continue to study tigers' behavior, habitats, and populations, and note anything that could harm the animals. To track tigers, scientists use many different methods. Trained eyes can look for tiger markings—urine spray on trees, paw prints (called pugmarks), and fecal droppings. Modern technology allows scientists to place remote cameras in tigers' habitats, and tigers walking past the devices trigger the flashes. If scientists want to follow one particular tiger, it is captured using a snare, then tranquilized and fitted with a radio collar.

There are also plans to introduce tigers born in captivity into the wild. Wild tiger populations are endangered,

Tigers that live on protected reserves are bred to produce cubs that will be reintroduced to the wild.

Although a tiger's sharp eyesight can expertly track prey's every move, scientists believe the cats cannot distinguish between colors very well.

but up to four times as many tigers live in captivity. It is not easy to introduce a tiger into the wild, as it needs to quickly learn the necessary survival skills. Some rare South China tigers have been bred in captivity and now live on a reserve in South Africa. Chinese scientists hoped that the tigers would be relocated to China by 2008 to coincide with the Olympic Games in Beijing, when the world's attention would be turned to the country.

Despite efforts to conserve the tiger, it still faces many threats. The tiger's biggest threat is not other animals, but humans. Humans **encroach** upon tiger habitat, overhunt traditional tiger prey, and, perhaps most significantly, continue to kill tigers for their skin and body parts.

Under the Convention on International Trade in Endangered Species of Wild Fauna and Flora (CITES) treaty, which was signed by 170 countries in 1973, it is illegal to trade and sell tiger body parts. However, poachers still sell fur, skins, teeth, and claws. Tiger bones, urine, teeth, and gall bladders are bought for use in making some ancient Asian medicines.

Tigers are today protected by law in all countries in which they live. However, enforcing those laws is another matter. It is impossible to watch every tiger all of the time, and poachers take advantage of this. They accept the risk of being caught because they are unwilling to give up the thousands of dollars they can earn for selling tiger body parts.

The untimely death of one tiger can affect the entire population in an area. A female that is killed is one less female that can breed. If a mother is killed, her young cubs will surely die. A male taken out of his territory leaves fewer choices for females when it comes time to mate.

Many tiger populations are isolated from one another due to spikes in human population. Half the world's population—more than 3 billion people—is found in the 13 countries in which tigers live. Forests and other traditional tiger habitats are routinely cleared for homes and farmland. People hunt the same animals that tigers do. Tigers are forced to move into smaller areas, which means that animals from the same family may end up breeding with each other. This results in sickly tigers with genetic problems caused by **inbreeding**.

Governments, researchers, and organizations are taking many measures to protect the tiger. One way to do so is to

Even though the cats face endangerment and extinction, tigers have not lost their playful attitudes.

protect its habitat and the species it feeds upon. At times, villagers who live within wildlife reserves are encouraged to relocate. The government gives them new land and resources such as drinking water, electricity, and health care, which they might not otherwise have access to.

Many protection measures center on the farmers who kill tigers that attack livestock. Conservationists encourage farmers to lock up their livestock at night instead of letting them roam free. Tigers are less likely to come near a village if they cannot find an easy food source there. Governments also pay villagers to leave tigers alone instead of shooting them.

Many organizations are dedicated to conserving tiger populations. The Save the Tiger Fund was formed in 1995 and is supported by ExxonMobil, the U.S. Fish and Wildlife Service, and the Disney Foundation. Other organizations include the Siberian Tiger Conservation Association and Wildlife Warriors Worldwide.

The good news is that, even with increases in human population, there are still reserves dedicated to tigers. Tiger populations appear to be healthiest in far eastern Russia and India. Southeast Asia also has the capability to

keep tiger populations stable or to increase them.

Throughout its history, the tiger has shown a remarkable will to survive. It even managed to survive throughout the 20th century, when hunting and poaching reduced its numbers to the point of extinction. With some help from conservationists, it is hoped that the tiger can find a safe, valued place in this shrinking world.

As long as tigers continue to breed and cubs are born, the world will not lose this special animal.

ANIMAL TALE: HOW THE TIGER GOT ITS STRIPES

Throughout history, stories have focused on how certain animals look the ways they do. This tiger tale comes from Vietnam and explains one theory of how the tiger got its stripes. The legend imparts the moral that it is best to be content with what you have and not to become too greedy.

One day, a farmer and his water buffalo were plowing a rice paddy. The farmer took a lunch break and rested beside a tree. The water buffalo lazily drank from a pond but soon became alarmed. He could sense a predator approaching. Before he knew it, a tiger appeared before him.

"Don't be afraid," the tiger said. "I come in peace. I've been watching you, and I've wondered why you obey the farmer's command each day. You are much larger than he is, and you could run away or even trample him. What kind of power does he hold over you?"

"I don't know about his power," the water buffalo said. "All I know is that he says he has this thing called wisdom, and as long as he has wisdom, I shall never be free."

The tiger thought for a moment. "I should like to have some of that wisdom. You see, I already have great power in the forest, but I would like even more. Instead of having to wait and sneak up on animals, with wisdom I could simply approach them and kill them whenever I wanted. I could have a great feast every day."

The water buffalo replied, "Why don't you ask the farmer about his wisdom?

Maybe he would be happy to share it with you."

The tiger approached the farmer. "Oh, wise man, I see the wisdom that you have and the power you hold over creatures. I would like some of that, too. Would you share it with me?"

"I don't have the wisdom right here," the farmer said. "I left it up at the house. I can get it for you."

"Oh, that would be wonderful," the tiger said. "Could I come with you?"

"No, I would prefer that you stay here. But I am concerned that while I am gone, you might try to eat my water buffalo. Would you mind if I tied you to this tree while you wait?"

The tiger, so desperate to receive the farmer's wisdom, agreed. The farmer used strong twine to tie up the tiger.

The farmer went to his house and got some straw. He brought it back to the tree, set it underneath the tiger, and lit it on fire.

"What are you doing?" the tiger cried. "I thought you were going to bring me wisdom!"

"Wisdom is so powerful that only I can hold it," the farmer said. "I cannot trust you with it."

The tiger howled as the fire roared around him. Finally, the fire burned through the rope and the tiger leapt away to the forest to lick his wounds. The burning ropes had seared into his fur, and the dark scars never went away. And that is how the tiger got its stripes.

GLOSSARY

bounties – payments or awards, especially from a government, for killing predatory animals

camouflaged – hidden, due to coloring or markings that blend in with a given environment

carcass – the dead body of an animal, especially one that will be used for food

colonies – territories that are claimed and ruled by another country

conservationist – a person who works to preserve a natural resource or wild animal

den – a secluded spot in which an animal raises its babies, lives, and sleeps

encroach – to intrude gradually into the space of another; going beyond prescribed boundaries

gladiator – an ancient Roman fighter who performed in front of large crowds, often fighting until he was killed in the arena

icons – images that are generally associated with one subject

inbreeding – the practice of individuals that are closely related mating; this can result in offspring with genetic problems or mutations

litter – babies that are born at the same time to animals such as dogs, cats, lions, and tigers

logos – images or groups of words that come to be associated with a particular thing

poachers – people who hunt protected species of wild game and fish, even though doing so is against the law

regal – having a graceful and proud appearance; a word usually associated with kings and queens

retract – to draw back

zoologist – a person who studies zoology, the biological discipline that involves the study of animals

SELECTED BIBLIOGRAPHY

Ashby, Ruth. *Jane Goodall's Animal World: Tigers*. New York: Atheneum, 1990.

Bortolotti, Dan. *Tiger Rescue*. Buffalo, NY: Firefly Books, 2003.

Corrigan, Patricia, Kathy Feeney, Gwyneth Swain, and Cherie Winner. *Big Cats*. Chanhassen, Minn.: NorthWord Press, 2002.

DuTemple, Lesley A. *Tigers*. Minneapolis: Lerner Publications, 1996.

Karanth, K. Ullas. *The Way of the Tiger*. Stillwater, Minn.: Voyageur Press, 2001.

National Fish and Wildlife Association. "Save the Tiger Fund." National Fish and Wildlife Association. http://www.savethetigerfund.org.

At birth and as adults, white tigers tend to be larger than their orange-colored counterparts.

INDEX